D1518730

POSSUMS aren't ICKY

by Wonky Kat Comix

WONKY KAT

www.wonkykat.com

Possums aren't icky.
The Virginia opossum is a weird and amazing masterpiece. If you see one in your sculpture garden, don't panic. They are on neighborhood watch for pests.

Possums are bug lovers.
Our possum pals like the finest of
bugs, dining on pesky pests like
spiders, roaches, and even lice.
The crunchier the better!
Bon Appétit!

Possums aren't rodents.
They are a breed of trash cat.
Possums and cats get along well.
Wonky Kat is Biscuit's best friend,
and the two often socialize over
pizza, cookies, or tea.

Possums are good neighbors.
They sleep through the day
and wander at night.
Biscuit is quiet and won't
throw house parties.

Possums are supportive moms, as they do not eat their young when frustrated with them. Being a marsupial, this North American possum has a pouch and can carry up to nine babies at a time.

Possums are scavengers. They're the ultimate snack-time enthusiasts, taking your leftovers and turning them into midnight munchies. Biscuit enjoys some good trash can mystery meat now and then!

Possums are very dramatic. They are known for playing dead. Don't sneak up on them, or they will give the worst performance of a lifetime.

Possums aren't gross.
They keep a neat, cat-like
routine. Biscuit makes sure
she washes from her ears to
her little possum feet.

Possums are introverted and don't like too much attention. They have social anxiety, so eye contact is the enemy. If you stare too long, Biscuit isn't sure what to do.

Possums are amazing climbers. They have the agility of a feline, being able to climb up into trees and make little nests where they can. The cost of rent for their nests is very low.

Possums have strong tails.
Even though they mostly sleep and
hide, they've got serious muscles
and a tail that is perfect for
picking fresh apples.

Possums aren't icky.
Though they may seem scary, when left alone, they are harmless. Just like all creatures on planet Earth, they are meant to be. As long as bugs and trash exist they are here to stay!

Thank you for reading!

For more content on Biscuit
and her friends, please visit:

www.wonkykat.com

Made in the USA
Coppell, TX
16 September 2023

21657916R00021